THE
DUFFER'S
GUIDE TO
COARSE FISHING

Mike Gordon

COLUMBUS BOOKS
LONDON

Other books in the Duffer's series:
The Official Duffer's Rules of Golf (John Noble)
The Official Duffer's Rules of Tennis (Bob Adams)
The Duffer's Guide to Golf: A Second Slice (Gren)
The Duffer's Guide to Rugby (Gren)
The Duffer's Guide to Cricket (Gren)
The Duffer's Guide to Greece (Gren)
The Duffer's Guide to Spain (Gren)

Copyright © 1985 Mike Gordon

First published in Great Britain in 1985 by
Columbus Books
Devonshire House, 29 Elmfield Road, Bromley, Kent BR1 1LT

Printed and bound by Clark Constable,
Edinburgh, London, Melbourne

ISBN 0 86287 176 X

Author's note:
My sincerest thanks to
my wife Maria and
to Mr Terry Sanders
for their invaluable help
(any resemblance to them by any characters portrayed
within is, of course, entirely incidental and completely
unintentional).

Fishing duffers can be hard to spot. After all, fishing is a mainly solitary sport, hardly suitable for spectators, and is often practised in the most remote areas.

Fishermen do not need to excel in anything athletic: all they require is a natural resistance to exposure, a rod, beanie hat and pair of wellies. Thus equipped, who's to know you've not been at it since you flushed Charlie Goldfish to the freedom of the cesspit?

More than any other of his kind, the fishing duffer has a wide margin on results, from the one that got away to the crispy golden ones wrapped in newspaper.

So, if the sight of a pair of scales, more than one fisherman or the appearance of any quarry over 6 inches long makes you nervous, this is the guide for you.

CONTENTS

Introduction

There are a number of bugs known to prey on mankind, the bite of which, once received, turns the victim into a Jekyll and Hyde character, who shows at times all the symptoms of normal civilized man (pays his bills and taxes, wears a suit and tie, cleans inside his ears, wears sober socks and underwear, etc.) but who at other times would be certified insane by even the most primitive bush doctor.

One such bug is the love-bug (*Mosca amicus*), whose bite causes drooling, day-dreaming, clumsiness with sharp objects, intermittent catalepsy, loss of appetite, and renders the victim totally incapable of interesting conversation, much given to interminable monologues on the desirability of a certain person or persons.

Second only to the love-bug (though some modern researchers claim that it is stronger) is *Mosca piscatoris*, the fishing-bug. Once bitten, the unfortunate victim rises at ungodly hours, tramps river, lock and canal banks while mist is yet rising from the surface, and stays until late into the night, whipping the water with a rod and lash (though the poor water has done little enough to him), cursing loudly, and on occasion inadvertently hooking out submarine creatures – which, if of the edible type, are too small to take home, and if inedible are not allowed to be taken home.

The victim bitten by *Mosca piscatoris* haunts tackle shops muttering ritualistic chants such as 'Carbon fibre, Greenwell's Glory, Cock y Bondhin, groundbait gentles and keepnet'. The victim learns to become a stranger to the truth, a frequenter of low taverns, an imbiber of strong liquors and a keeper of ungodly hours.

Garbed in strange attire, he will leave the bosom of his family and, cleaving to men of like mind, will vanish for hours or even days, returning with cold feet, a red nose and something small and silvery which, when placed in a frying-pan, looks like a pimple on an elephant.

I know. I was that soldier.

Bitten on a canal-bank in Lancashire aged nine years. Have suffered ever since.

Mike Harding

Coarse Types

As the duffer prepares to take his place under the green umbrellas of the well-worn riverbank, he would do well to choose his pitch according to his would-be neighbour. Eccentricities abound in this one-man sport, but the following descriptions should help cast the duffer in the right direction.

1. The beginner

The most maddening traits are often found in the beginner. He'll be the one standing in his waders, in rushing flood waters, in everyone's way, with a five-foot rod and bright blue maggots, expecting to catch a 20-lb carp. Or he'll be six years old and do the same using his mum's nylons.

Most beginners start with a good chance of not ending up as duffers, but some are destined never to be anything else.

2. The match angler

Competition is the lifeblood of this type. Be sure to disregard any advice from a match angler. His tips are designed at the very least to lead an opponent astray, at worst to cast him to the murky depths forever.

Silent and cunning, he strives at all costs to stay ahead of the field in technique and gadgetry. He'll be the one you'll encounter in the tackle shop when his children are getting married or his wife is giving birth.

Duffers, steer clear.

8

3. The total failure

Legends of werewolves in certain localities are actually attributable to the total fishing failure. This one fishes only at night, so he feels free to let loose his wails and howls of rage. The total failure never catches a thing.

A charmer with the ladies, well-liked by the lads, does well at his job – nevertheless, this type is eaten up by his drive to succeed at his chosen hobby. Often ends up with only his dog for company – if he hasn't already tried using it for groundbait.

Duffers can find his fruitless efforts cheering, but be warned: his condition is contagious.

4. The carp fisherman

The completely crazed angler. The carp has him hooked, swallowed up in the world of the CAA. Not just any carp, but 'Wob', 'Bob', or 'Gerald', who turn every catch into a reunion. Here is the two-in-the-morning man whose wife, if she hasn't left him, crochets his keep nets.

Duffers, unless your socks produce a nice essence of apricot or rosy plum, or you possess some other highly secret bait ingredient, the carp angler's world is one about which you'll only dream.

10

5. The club angler

This one doesn't like to overstrain his drinking arm, so you'll never find him on the bank after opening time. Has to be dragged back on to the coach for home. Always the first to put his name down for an exchange trip with a German *biergarten* troop. Gave up serious thoughts of competition after his friends found him demonstrating the art of legering to the landlord's wife. Can provide the duffer with a lot of relief: the bottled kind.

Some Fishy Spots

The fishing duffer is often found wandering aimlessly around traffic islands, or you might encounter him on your next trip to the local tip. He'll be fully-equipped and anxiously searching for Fisherman's Paradise. Here we deal with the less luxurious spots that the duffer frequents, discovered more by accident than design.

COUGH COUGH

1. The pond

This is where mum goes walkies with the pram in which her ten manky little kids used to wee-wee, with the idea of discarding the said offspring in the deep. This is where you might find the beginner not quite ready to part with his money in licence fees. Why should he, when he can adorn his house with brass beads, bikes and a pair of pre-shrunk Wranglers? The pond is the starting place for all successful scrap-dealers — but certainly not anglers.

2. The golf course

These are absolutely littered with waterways, as all good sportsmen know. Sarcastic enquiries about your possible catch can be answered with the witty and simple retort, 'Balls!'. A pleasant spot as long as the duffer's reflexes are up to ducking the well-aimed 'head-in-one' shot.

3. The gravel-pit

The best are normally sited next to a funfair, between two motorways, on a seismic fault, and are well-stocked with deaf pike.

Only when the cold, hard steel of the bulldozer takes the earth from under him does the duffer realize nobody meant a *working* gravel-pit.

THIS IS THE PITS!

4. The reservoir

An upmarket gravel-pit. Particularly hazardous at certain times of the year when seasons overlap.

In case of undesired encounters, remember:

1. You got there first.
2. Wet breaking strain is probably reached at about 12 knots.

5. The bog

You get in a nice bit of still-water practice here. The duffer might be lucky and hook a bottom feeder, but it's doubtful he'll flush out anything big. Always good for a bit of peace and quiet.

The Catch,
and Other Unidentified
Floating Objects

It's a well-known fact that fishermen have the longest arms of any sportsmen. For, as any good duffer knows, it's not the type or quality of the catch, but the distance end to end (give or give a few inches) that matters. In fact, many a fish has been known to grow to amazing proportions after just a few beers.

The following are just a few duff specimens. Never mind the quality – feel the length!

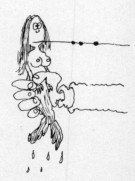

1. The freshwater wellie

This catch comes in several forms, from the shoefish to the sandal – in addition to the common wellie. In attempts to avoid embarrassment, the duffer has been known, on plucking one of these from the mud, to shout 'At last! I knew I lost it somewhere around here!' But there's really no disguising the fact that this haul is entirely inedible and always beyond the salvation of odour-eaters.

2. The lesser-spotted bike frame

A bottom feeder. Proves you can leger. Some claim they heard 'magnets' for 'maggots'. Usually takes several hours to land, giving the duffer a brief taste of the best of the sport until it suddenly reels into his teeth. Don't neglect to weigh this one in – it can make an impressive, if somewhat obscured, entry in your records.

3. The thing stuck to the bottom

This species may or may not release its hold on the bed. Indeed, it may be a bed. There are limitless variations, but most are undistinguishable and extremely smelly. Some can even put a club angler off his beer for a couple of hours. This is one catch you always throw back or keep for your mother-in-law.

21

4. The opponent's ear

Good to use when the know-it-all has just caught ten 2-lb roach in the last three minutes. Fasten a nice cold minnow, then cast vigorously over your shoulder. Ignore the first four-letter word and give the line a strong tug before turning in surprise. Apologize profusely, keep your distance and don't make any sick jokes about lobe worms making good bait. Then turn away and discreetly don your balaclava.

5. The worm

Usually the result of twelve patient hours with your best rod in the best spot for miles, the worst kind of this species comes out smaller than it went in.

6. The one that got away

Never mind the loud-mouthed arm-spreader going on about the one he lost. Look for the angler alone in the corner, the odd tear mingling with his tenth beer. This is the one whose 3-foot 10-lb chub suddenly jumped up after a two-hour struggle, raised two fins and bit through his line. It would kill him to tell his friends and the image will haunt his nights for the next year.

7. The real thing

Once in a while the duffer lands a fish. After hooking barbells, broom, wheels and Chubb locks, this comes as a mighty relief. Nothing can diminish a duffer's pride in the first 10-oz dace, even if it turns out to be a senile chub that limped in through a hole in his keep net.

8. The fish finger*

No bones about it, this must be the most inconvenient of all catches. The unfortunate duffer has to suffer many frustrating hours on the riverbank and an unsuccessful dash to the fishmonger only to find that all that's left is this ready-processed, pre-packaged excuse for the species.

* Not to be confused with Fisher's Finger (also known as Duffer's Sprain).

26

9. Mabel at the George and Dragon

This is just one of the species much sought-after but seldom caught. Wise to all the usual bait and often moving on to better prospects in other watering holes. Has proved the undoing of more than one duffer who made too free with his tackle.

Weather or Not

The seasoned duffer will soon learn to brave monsoons and hurricanes. He may even become an expert in the thunder technique for stunning fish, conducting lightning down his wilting rod. If not, he might not make it. But a duffer on his guard for the following conditions should be able to avoid rising damp, even if he's already got wet rot.

1. Down wind

There are two kinds of wind that irritate the angler: the force 10 and the internal, the latter erupting after eight pints and a vindaloo curry. Never tangle with either, especially the second. Remember, flatulence will get you nowhere.

2. Deep heat

Did you ever hear of a nomad hooking a 10-lb bream in the depths of the Sahara? Nor has anyone else. So, next time you start thinking you should pack your maggots, hooks and sinkers in an ice-box, think again and pack the Martini instead.

3. Cold (mark 7 on your freezer)

Some fish don't mind it a bit on the cold side. Not so the fisherman, wrapped in woollies and long johns, who jiggles and shivers on the river-bank in front of a six-inch hole cut in the ice. There is a rumour that intense cold cracks the lead shot on your line, so you lose it to the fast-flowing river. Be assured though, whatever you've heard, that your balls do not actually drop off.

4. Sinking in the rain

One duffer was known to complain to his land-lord about the beer being a bit cloudy. 'What do you want for 80p? Thunder and bl**dy light-ning?!' was the reply. This is exactly what the good duffer wants. So never be surprised when you see hordes of anglers making for the river like drowned rats, in thermal underwear, pack-ing little green umbrellas.

5. The peasouper

Old Granny is going to see herself packed off to the loony bin if she makes any more complaints about her camisoles and corsets being plucked from her washing line and flying through the air. There are also tales of rancid monster fish leaping out of the swirling mists, all clammy and drooling. But this is probably the duffer's first sight (just before he passed out) of the slightly inebriated search party comprised of those who realized he's missed his round that evening.

Then again, the duffer should always wipe his specs: this may clear up everything instantly.

33

Hook, Line and Stinker (the Fisherman's Tackle)

Guarded lovingly, this can grow out of all proportion. About the only straightforward bit, however, is the wellie boot. So, if you feel a little pre-angling try-out is needed and next door's dog keeps peeing on your lawn, invite your neighbour over and innocently invite him to experiment with your disgorgers and gaffs.

Even if you've no idea what it's for – buy it. You never know when you might have to unpick the cat's stitches or remove a wart. Whatever else you pack, though, be sure not to miss the following essentials.

1. Rods: stiff, limp and collapsible

The rod is not a lasso. If some other duffer should shout 'Tonto!' he's either calling his dog or has just landed a 40-lb carp on his foot. An instrument of precision, an extension of the bloke on the bank, a fine match rod can bring tears to the eye – especially when it belongs to your opponent. So spare no expense: if necessary, hire someone to remove his spigots or 'adjust' his rings.

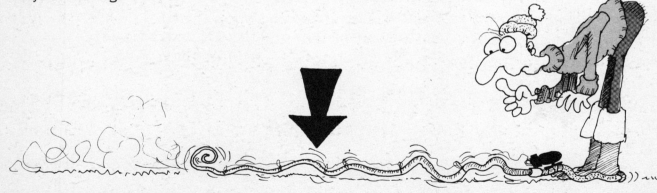

2. The shotgun

This comes equipped with its own 12-bore bait. Used with a barrel, it is a sure-fire way for the duffer to succeed. It's also useful for game-keeper impersonations when you want a good spot to yourself (and excellent for relieving pent-up frustrations about the ones that got away).

3. 'Thar' she blows!'
Harpoon: the bait-less rod

Harpoons are great for when a flock of mangy old crows have eaten the last of your bread paste while some whopper just swam off with your No. 2. Simply swing back with your casting arm and heave it in the same direction as the hook. You may or may not have shortened the odds of making your catch, but it's odds on that no one else will make it – or their own – at least until the last ripple has gone. As the harpoon is actually regarded as a little antisocial, it's best kept hidden and only used as a last resort.

THWACK

37

4. Medicinal tonic

Many a distressed angler keeps himself 98% proofed against the elements. The best tonic numbs the shock of your worst catch in weeks, takes the chill out of frost-bite and makes even your neighbour's 39-lb pike seem laughable. The duffer should always carry some of this in the knowledge that fishermen rarely rate rescue by St Bernard dogs.

5. Thing for taking stones out of horses' hooves

Easily obtainable with just a bag of gob-stoppers shoved under the local cub scouts' noses. Very useful when you've forgotten your hanky.

39

6. The dock leaf

Good for wasp and nettle stings, but especially useful for when you're caught short. Not a patch on Andrex, but still strong, soft and very plentiful.

40

7. Electronic aids

Don't go overboard here. Forty-eight hours of constant echo-sounding with an extension lead on the car battery or the nearest pylon is not advised, not if you want to get home again. But there's a lot to be said for the electronic bite indicator, especially if it can be rigged up to Dolly Parton singing 'Yellow Rose of Texas' played through your personal stereo earplugs (guaranteed to rouse the drowsiest duffer). And don't get caught, like one duffer, trying to tune into the weather forecast with his straight antennae.

8. Rest and clamp

A good combination. On steep banks it's best to clamp before you rest, firmly securing outer garments to the nearest solid object to avoid a wet and slippery awakening when a passing barge takes a fancy to your maggot.

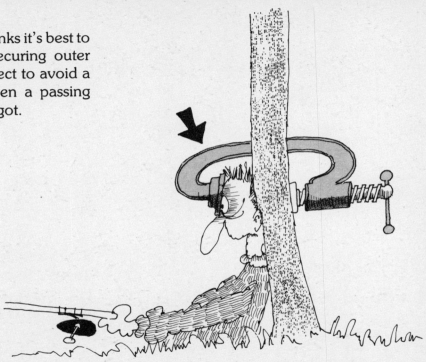

9. The tackle box

This holds all the angler's treasures. Never use large, fancy-coloured ones as these stick out too much on the bank. Stay with the traditional well-balanced design into which everything fits snugly.

43

Off-coarse Zones

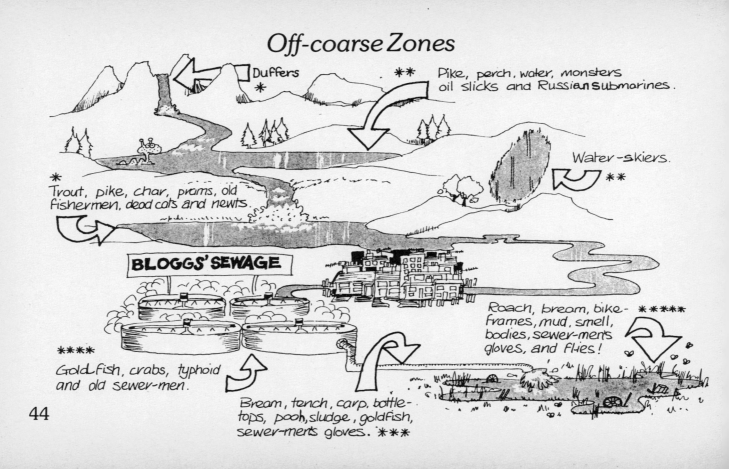

Duffers

Pike, perch, water, monsters oil slicks and Russian submarines. **

Water-skiers. **

Trout, pike, char, prams, old fishermen, dead cats and newts. *

BLOGGS' SEWAGE

Roach, bream, bike-frames, mud, smell, bodies, sewer-men's gloves, and flies! *****

Goldfish, crabs, typhoid and old sewer-men. ****

Bream, tench, carp, bottle-tops, pooh, sludge, goldfish, sewer-men's gloves. ***

44

The Off-coarse Fisherman

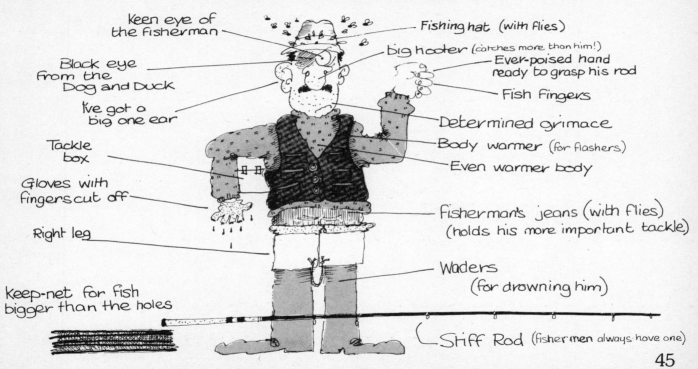

Keen eye of the fisherman

Fishing hat (with flies)

Black eye from the Dog and Duck

big hooter (catches more than him!)

Ever-poised hand ready to grasp his rod

I've got a big one ear

Fish Fingers

Tackle box

Determined grimace

Body warmer (for flashers)

Even warmer body

Gloves with fingers cut off

Fisherman's jeans (with flies) (holds his more important tackle)

Right leg

Waders (for drowning him)

keep-net for fish bigger than the holes

Stiff Rod (fishermen always have one)

45

Throwing Wobblies and Wrigglies

From finding nice, fat juicy ones to little wrigglers, worm-digging and grubbing for maggots are almost sports on their own, giving the true enthusiast something to get his teeth into. The angler meets a hive of seething activity as he delves into some of these exotic delicacies. Clue up on the following basics and you'll have no trouble tempting fish or identifying the contents of any dubious take-away.

1. The worm

Legless, like the club angler, this species revels in places damp, dark and degenerate. The major cause behind compost heaps quaking in the night and feeble-eyed Aunty's screams as she takes the lid off what was once the marmalade jar.

2. Grub's up

It certainly is – and all over your best gear, too, when you find a gozzer dropped in your sandwiches.

48

3. Mother's pride

There are two possibilities: the soft, white, starchy stuff that comes in slices, or the little monster responsible for gluing them all together with raspberry jam. In fact, who knows what might be achieved with a touch of preserve on the bait, or cream cheese, pickled ham, fried egg, tomato sauce or some salmon spread?

Go on – experiment. Where the butty begins, a fish may end.

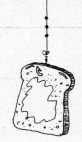

4. Greenbottle pinkies

These can be feeder maggots, but there is a distilled version encountered by the rather merry angler: namely, the way his fingers look through the bottle of gin he's just finished.

5. Kids and cats

These items can be your own or somebody else's. Use these as a last resort when your catch has just disappeared between whiskered jaws, or after five biteless hours of being gawped at, or when you're sure it's bubblegum that's got your maggots glued to the lid.

51

6. Spinners, spoons and wobbly baits

Too many of these from this man-made section and your tackle box will sound as if you've just won the main prize on a one-armed bandit. So don't waste your money on lots of fancy lures. Forks, knives or the club trophy – anything will do when you're desperate.

Sink or Swim, and Other Ways to Become a Happy Hooker

When the duffer goes trotting he wears out his wellies and wonders why nobody told him it was such an active sport. So, rather than complicate matters by discussing fly rods, laying-on, sink and draw tactics, etc., he would do better to stick to the following three basic techniques, all of which should come to him naturally.

1. Float fishing

Best from a prone position, with a snorkel to give a better chance of spotting the little blighters. This can prove a very unsuccessful method if you keep lead shot in your pockets, although it saves using your plummet.

2. Leg-ering

The size of catch here depends largely on your wellie capacity. There is a single-leg adaptation requiring more skill and a very well-balanced action. However, two legs, one wellie and no socks make for great live bait.

3. Spinning

This is really more of an after-angling entertainment, when tales of long-departed fish and fishermen can be spun out for hours. Based firmly in fiction, the very best yarns are told by spinners who can make the existence of an over-sized, fag-smoking pike with B.O. and a London accent seem a distinct possibility.

WAFFLE WAFFLE . . .
WAFFLE WAFFLE WAFFLE
WAFFLE WAFFLE, WAFFLE
WAFFLE WAFFLE, WAFFLE
WAFFLE WAFFLE WAFFLE
WAFFLE WAFFLE WAFFLE . .
. . . WAFFLE WAFFLE
WAFFLE WAFFLE WAFFLE
WAFFLE WAFFLE WAFFLE
WAFFLE WAFFLE

YAWN!

YAWN!

YAWN!

Tips and Definitions

No angling duffer can get by without at least a sprinkling of technical terms and a hint of expertise. Reserve your tip of the day until the sixth round and no one will realize it came from this book.

1. Fish can grow to extraordinary proportions in areas where the water is kept at artificially high temperatures.

Breaking strain: time to cart you away.

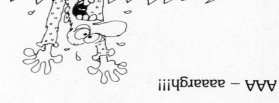

AAA – aaaarghi!!

2. Polarized sunglasses can help you see under water.

Dry flies: where you manage to keep out of the water.

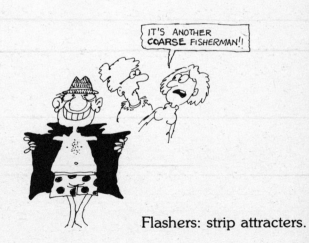

IT'S ANOTHER **COARSE** FISHERMAN!!

Flashers: strip attracters.

3. A large lure can prove an effective decoy in
drawing large specimens.

Taking short: using everybody else's dock leaves as well as your own.

Terminal rig: (1) what you've got on your end. (2) (-or mortis) total paralysis from standing for eight hours in the pouring rain.

4. When legering, fix a butt indicator to the rear end to signal a bite.

Troll: very ugly fisherman.

Zoomer: camera lens for observing female of the species.

5. Organization into clubs or groups can mean a discount on those large purchases of essential tackle.

Strike: blow delivered to your opponent.

Slurry: residual deposits in your pint pot.

Duffers' Dos and Don'ts

Do keep the names and addresses of a couple of reliable witnesses who will swear that the frozen core of your record-beating catch was due to inclement weather and not your freezer at the time of hooking.

Don't give up in a match: you never know when your usual stickleback may just win the day.

Don't congratulate your fellow angler with a pat on the back – he could well be warming his maggots.

Do take care not to trespass.

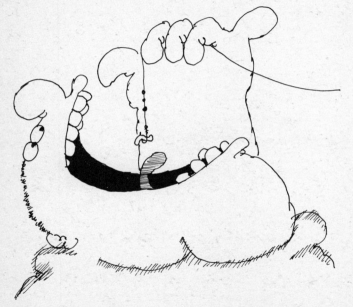

Don't eat the bait, even when you've forgotten the sandwiches.

Don't daydream – you might just lose your tackle.

Do use both hands when landing your opponent.

Don't try to fiddle the peg draw – this will have been done already.

Do avoid unseemly disputes between your fellows — be sure to specify who gets your tackle when you finally depart for Pikers' Paradise.

Do tell Mummy where you're going.